AF585117

MY REAL DOG

BY EMILY JOE

Some kids wish for brand new bikes,
for fancy dolls or belts with spikes

But as for me, I've always known
I need a dog to call my own.

But my parents sure do
make a fuss
on why a dog's not right for us
The house is small,
The time's not right,

It'll bark and bark right through the night
Theyre smelly, and hairy, and make me sneeze
and not to mention those horrid fleas!

But little do my parents know,
I got a real dog long ago.

He's fairly small, and sometimes stiff
With big dark eyes and a nose to sniff

He's got black spots

one

two

three

And he wags his tail
(with help from me)

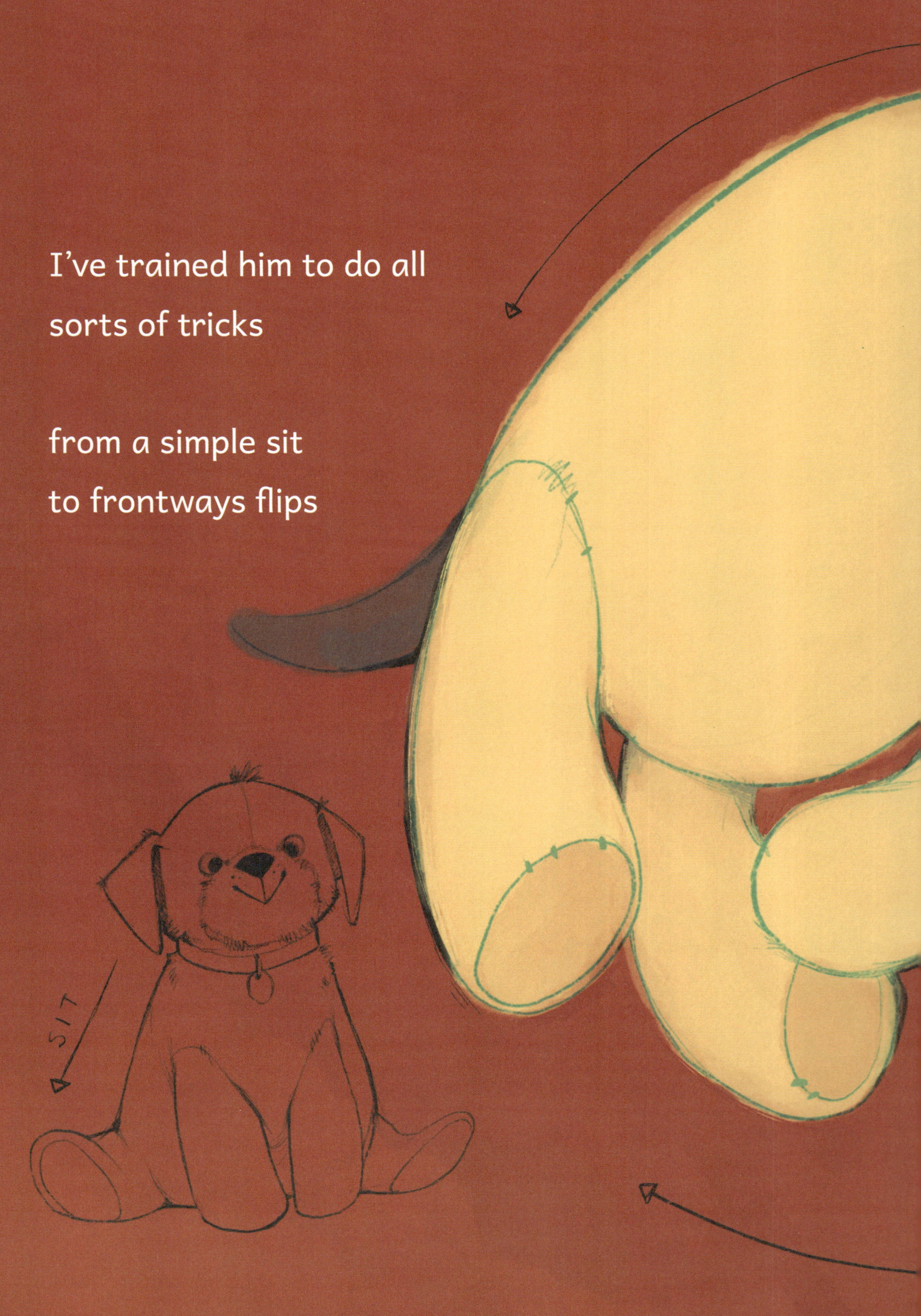
I've trained him to do all
sorts of tricks

from a simple sit
to frontways flips
SIT

And when I tell
him just to
STAY
He's completely still
for the whole day.

And when we all sit down to eat,
he knows not to beg me for a treat.

No matter what is on my plate,
He'll always look, but never take.

And wait to see how fast he can zoom,

dashing behind me from room to room

Jumping

and

leaping

then coming to stop,

On the foot of my bed

with a soft fluffy

Each night you'll find him in my bed,
keeping watch right beside my head.
Because nothing makes me quite so calm,
as when he's tucked beneath my arm.

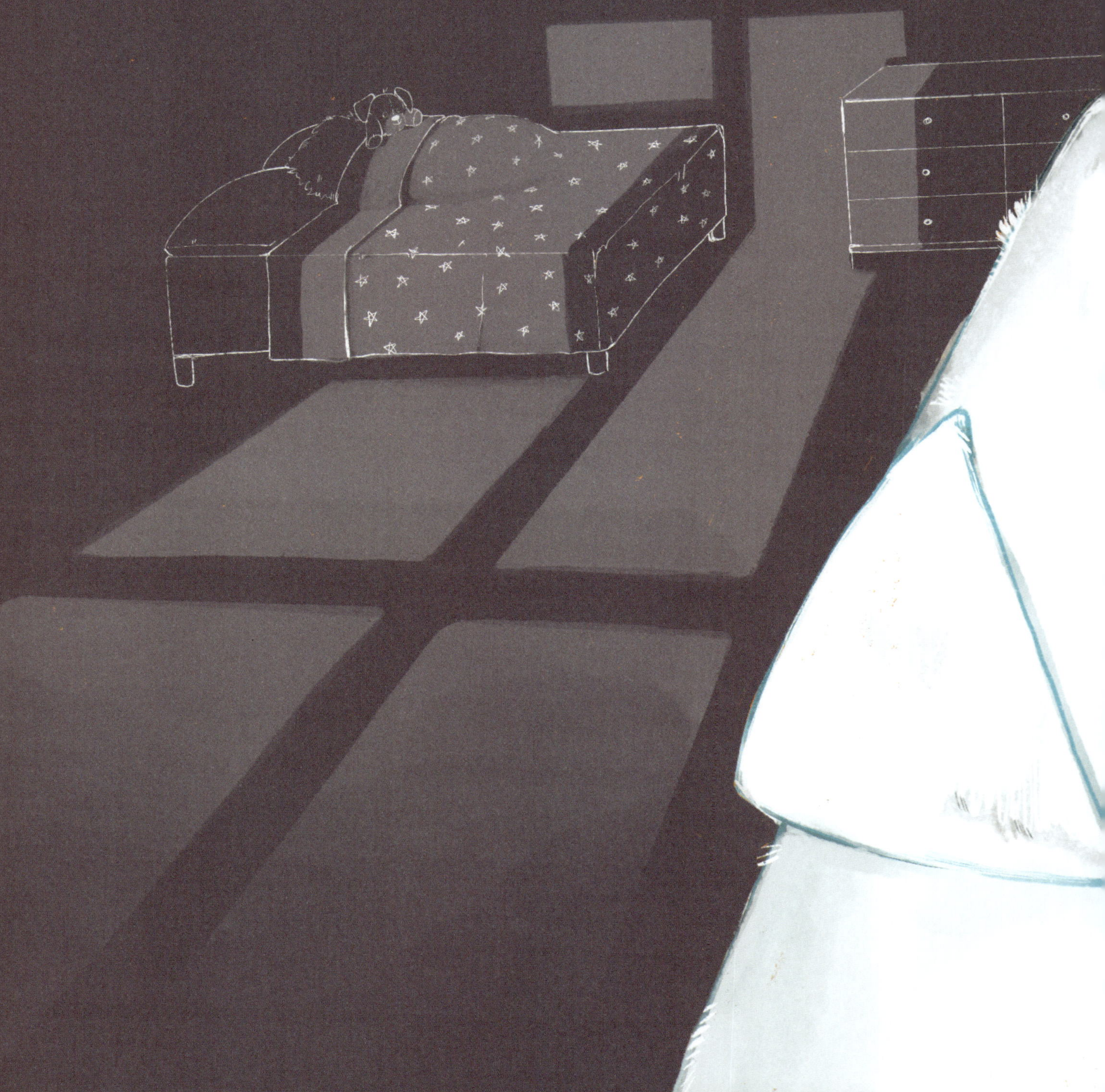

And what's more, he doesn't bark
Or roll in smelly things in the park
Or chew, or bite, or disobey,
And I know he'd never run away.

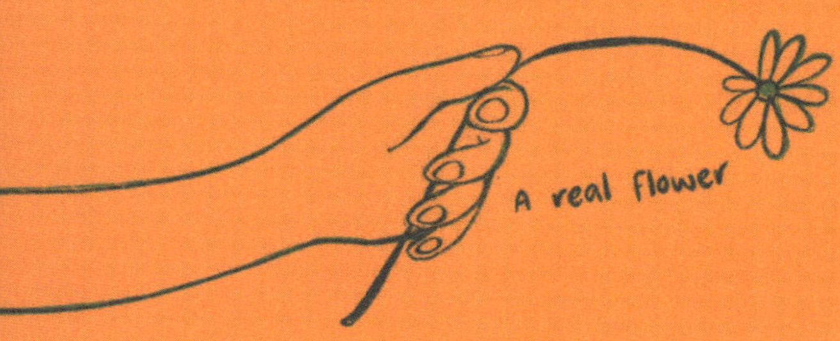

You'll find my dog is just as real,
as anything else I can see or feel.

He may not blink or bark – but I don't mind,
a toy's just a dog of a different kind.

No matter whether or not
your dog is a toy,

if they're fluffy or smooth,
a good girl or boy,

or giant and floppy,
with great hairy paws...

The best dog of all
is the one that is yours.

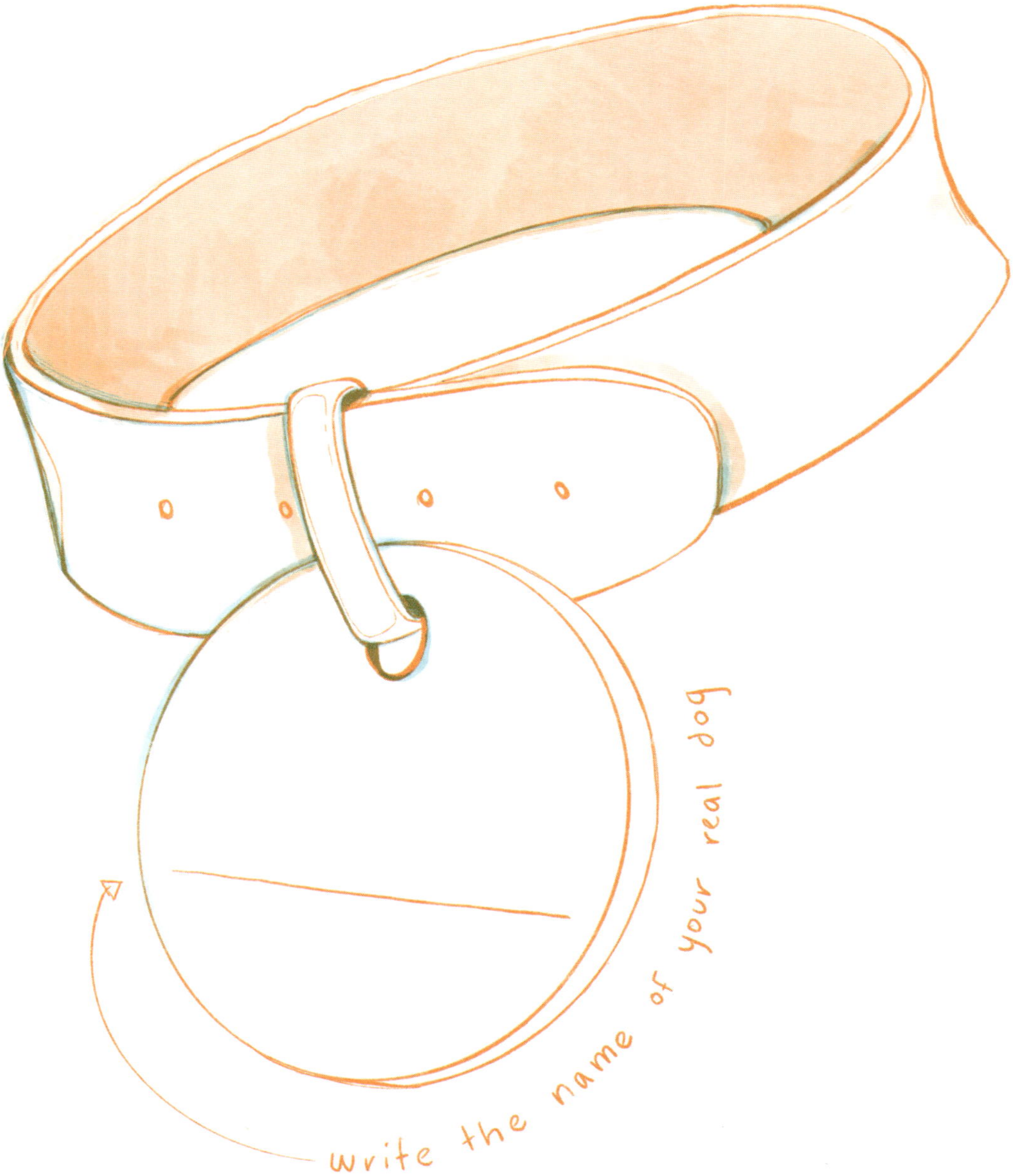

write the name of your real dog

Beatnik

PO Box 8276, Symonds Street,
Auckland 1150, New Zealand.

First published in 2022 by Beatnik Publishing.

Printed and bound in China.

ISBN 978-1-99-116570-1